Praise for OUI

"Bold. Healing. Generous. In this chronicling, Maureen Kwiat Meshenberg leads us through the spiraling between suffering and beauty, a ritual of being expressed through poetry. I love the ways this collection experiments with form in a time when the world seems to resist form. And so, as she writes, *let us become, let us become, let us become.*"

    —ROSEMERRY WAHTOLA TROMMER, author of *Hush, Naked for Tea* and *Even Now*

"In a time of great uncertainty and unrest, Maureen's poetry is a balm to the soul. Her words flow with gentle hope, capturing the beauty of our shared human experience, offering us a way through our collective suffering. It is a rare gift when an artist can lift our spirit and return us to the heart with such eloquence and grace, as Maureen does so generously."

    —FLORA AUBE, visual artist

"These poems sprung from the tender intersection of revolution and vulnerability, where Maureen Kwiat Meshenberg lyrically chronicles the unpredictable landscape of the pandemic for thirty courageous days. Moved by humanity coming to an external halt, Maureen enters into rich, internal conversations with her own heart, some of her favorite authors, and achy remembrances of pre-quarantine freedoms. From hopeful haikus to rhythmic couplets, we're led through beautiful existential explorations, trickling out in pink moons, deep breaths, pregnant horizons, colorful kaleidoscopes, and Roman holidays. Like comforting rituals and hugs for these times of grief, each poem softly yields to the opportunity of finding sacredness in the pause and treating oneself with compassion. Whether it's in yellow Daffodils, a sign spotted in a neighbor's window, magical runes, or Bodhisattva love-vows, Maureen's poetry reflects the possibilities that lie ahead of us and within us, with a gentle reminder that we are all at the dawn of a soulful recovery. This—Maureen's second collection of poems—reads like a tribute to our resilience, to our indisputable interconnectedness, to loving no matter what. In the author's own words: *When you see the thin line break, love comes for us.*

—CATHERINE L. SCHWEIG, Founder of Journey of the Heart Project, Editor of the award-winning *Goddess—When She Rules: Expressions by Contemporary Women*

"Maureen's latest collection of poetry brings balm for the soul at a much needed time. Whether read straight through or a page every day, it's the kind of book that you want to keep close by. There is an encompassing of all the deep and challenging feelings everyone has been faced with during this pandemic, leaving the reader feeling gently supported and not so alone. There is a deep sense of hope and universal gratitude felt in every page. I know this book will offer so many great comfort."

—TRACY ANN BROOKS, Founder of Soul Beckons, author of newly released book *Peace on Your Path*

"Maureen Kwiat Meshenberg's second collection *Our Surrendering Pause* is a meditation of spirit and a conscious deep writing practice that allows the reader into the mind of the poet's deepest *place of vulnerability and radical upheaval.* Writing during a time of unprecedented pause, not just personally, but on a planetary level during COVID–19, Meshenberg seizes the opportunity to raise a magnifying glass to her soul and look deeper within, questioning her own evolution and navigation through a completely new world— *what challenges us / creates our strength / through love's infinite voice.* And by tapping into that infinite voice, that urge toward awakening, the poems within inhale and exhale earthly and divine, longing and letting go, releasing and renewing. *Our Surrendering Pause* taps the reader on the shoulder and says, *build me a bridge/ to the universe,* and with each turn of the page, the heart and spirit rise to the stars."

—KAI COGGIN, author of *Wingspan*, *Incandescent* and *Periscope Heart*

Our Surrendering Pause

Our Surrendering Pause

30 Poems in 30 Days

MAUREEN KWIAT MESHENBERG

2020
GOLDEN DRAGONFLY PRESS

FIRST PRINT EDITION, July 2020
FIRST EBOOK EDITION, July 2020
1 2 3 4 5 6 7 8 9 10

ISBN–13: 978-1-7330099-2-8

Library of Congress Control Number: 2020941656

Printed on acid-free paper supplied by a
Forest Stewardship Council-certified provider.
First published in the United States of America
by Golden Dragonfly Press, 2020.

www.goldendragonflypress.com

www.facebook.com/Heartcalling

This book is dedicated to the many doctors, nurses and essential workers, saving and helping the lives of many, all over the world.

This book is also dedicated to my family, to my twin sister Marianne for inspiring me to write this book of poetry.

To my children Alexandra, Dylan, and Jonah for helping me shop and being there for me during this pandemic as I live alone.

To my many readers.
Lastly to my dog Tsuki, who brings me unfounded joy through our walks together during this pandemic.

CONTENTS

FOREWORD

This world needs more poetry and *Our Surrendering Pause* brings it to us. Maureen spent thirty days writing thirty poems to encapsulate a period where the entire world has been experiencing a viral pandemic—COVID–19. During her contemplative isolation, Maureen shares herself through a daily process of poetry. Her words are as soothing as honey is to tea. Each poetic offering is the very pause and soul nourishment we need.

Her words lead us to find rest and to honor our self during this time of unease. She shares with us her creative intelligence through her poetic chambers of self-love as if painting a cloud for us to sleep on. In her poem "The Distance Between" Maureen succinctly expresses herself with this poignant stanza:

> *The distance between*
> *you and me*
> *life and death*
> *beauty and pain*
> *we spiral between*
> *the edges of us.*

Maureen leaves nothing undiscovered and leads us eloquently into a prose-poem titled, "Create Me a Kaleidoscope of Colors," where we are swept away into an almost fairy tale:

"I catch blue with my eyes and with surprise, iridescently cracks the sky with yellow slipping between ethereal clouds of rest." What stunning imagery! I can taste it.

Each poem is a glimpse of how sentiments are an ebb and flow of the sea. We need our emotions to navigate and Maureen demonstrates this fluidly in "Colors."

> *I fell into blue*
> *clouds waiting for an*
> *invitation to sleep,*
> *waiting and wanting to just*
> *receive a resting call to lay endlessly.*

Maureen carries the reader through a continuous rainbow of vulnerability and lets each emotion feel valid and seen; you will sense her love for humanity.

This collection of thirty poems in thirty days is a treasure to turn to again and again.

Thank you, Maureen, for your indelible poetic ink.

Carolyn M. Riker, MA, LMHC
Issaquah, Washington
June 2020

INTRODUCTION

"I see our brilliant hearts
pilgrims on this journey we are
to open up our inviting hearts
a self-folding into self
our surrendering pause."

When something eclipses your life, bringing you to your void, a surrendering pause; physically, emotionally spiritually, what is your response? When something formidable happens and we feel the edges of our vulnerability stretch, will it bring us to our brave, our light, to grace?

What often offers itself to us isn't always something we want to accept. We want to retreat, find our way back to what was, back to our normalcy. We find that when we are brought to groundlessness, to our transformation, what is always changing, we have two choices. We can bring ourselves to awakening or resume to our old ways and habits, pushing it away or deep down inside of us. I have been through many awakening and groundless horizons, enough to bear witness to me transforming into a prolific poet. Words spoken from the soul, transforming the heart and uplifting the mind. These horizons of transformation have always brought me to my inner well of words that spill onto the page and bring inspiration and solace at the same time.

My writing journey began in 2011 and has been my lightwork since. When I first heard about April being National Poetry Month, I first was invited by a Writing Magazine called, *Tifferet Journal*, to take the challenge to writing a new poem each day for 30 days for the month of April (2015, 2016). The editor would give us challenging writing prompts each day to write a new poem. I did their challenge for two years, then started my own challenge through my Facebook page *Heart's Calling*. I would do it for charity such as Sarah's Inn: A shelter for domestic violence against women and children.

Coming into 2020, I could have not imagined what was unfolding before us. This pandemic is one of those things that eclipses our lives. This April, writing through the pandemic, brought me to the place of vulnerability and radical upheaval. I also saw, I was not alone. I challenged myself to write a new poem every day, most of them as works of inspiration as we all moved through this unprecedented time in history. As my poems unfolded every day, my twin sister Marianne approached me and said, *"Maureen, you should write a book of your poems during this pandemic."*

I realized, not only did I want my poems to be in print, to uplift and inspire many, but I also wanted the proceeds from the book to go to COVID–19 Relief. This is how my journey began with writing this book.

As I have seen many who have gone through great losses, loss of loved ones and friends, including myself, I hold a tender place of grace and sacred prayers for them. As I have seen the doctors, the nurses and essential workers, work on the frontlines to help humanity through this crisis, my heart moves deeply for their dedication. As I have seen the changes we are challenged to move through, I look it as a time of *Our Surrendering Pause,* a time for deep reflection as we move through this offering of transformation. Can we allow it to bring us to a deeper love, to a wider kindness, as we journey on this earth together? This is my hope, my resting belief, believing that the good will outweigh the bad. That we as a human race can comfort each other through this time of change. We have the choice to choose the power of love, and even through our vulnerability make a space in our lives to continually show that love to ourselves and to each other.

May my poems bring a sense of peace, inspiration, but most of all, love to you. Open the deep well inside you and let my words flow in.

A Haiku (breaking the rules)
Instead...a 7/5/7 rhythm
5 stanzas

I Hold

I hold a flower called time
petals fall to earth
blending with soil dissolving

I hold the sky with silence
I slip into grace
wind exhales her breath freely

I hold water like soft tears
falling from white clouds
night freeing them like bright stars

I hold melancholy close
my heart aches boldly
brave comes for me when I fall

I hold tomorrow with choice
colors catching me
prisms crack the window sky

Since Yesterday

since yesterday
the rain wept lonely loss
caught between
a thought and a dream
folding into hugging you
taking your hand in mine
since yesterday

since yesterday
I sat with wine in hand
conversing across from you
while people's chatter
filled the restaurant
with laughter
with memories
caught between
a thought and a dream
since yesterday

since yesterday
silence catches my breath
I sit by the window
and prayers press
upon my lips
caught between
a thought and a dream
life isn't always
what it seems
since yesterday

since yesterday
a walk outside
is a sweet luxury
child chalking
rainbows and notes
on sidewalks
caught between
a thought and a dream
that streams through
the waiting night
with brilliant stars
that have been with us
since yesterday

since yesterday
humanity cries
quiet hope shouts
and she will rise
what is caught between
a thought and a dream
our song
our mantra
our shouts
our cries
what challenges us
creates our strength
through love's infinite voice
for today
for forever
since yesterday

A rondel poem.

Spring Leans into the Warming Sky

spring leans into the warming sky
as the grass shifts into shades of green
whispering to the trees, "it's now spring!"
tulips tilt heads towards the sun so high

hummingbirds hum and the willow sighs
window ledge birds sing song sing
spring leans into the warming sky
as the grass shifts into shades of green

as thundering clouds, begin to cry
colors dance magic brilliant schemes
bursting brilliance like a fragrant dream
blooming rushes in, as winter now dies
spring leans into the warming sky.

The Distance Between

the distance between
life and death
beauty and pain
a prayer and a cry
a baby's lullaby
falling down and rising again,
falling and rising again
I rise again

I spiral between
the edges of me
interweaving through
in and out of me,
in and out of me
beginnings and endings
again and again

the seeing between
through my weary and strength
the drastic and mundane
through ordinary and riding
the tidal wave,
riding the tidal wave
again and again

the suffering between
the healing of it
the rumbling of the ache
the beauty of it all
that takes my breath away,

that takes my breath away
again and again

the distance between
you and me
life and death
beauty and pain
we spiral between
the edges of us
interweaving through
in and out of our living
our beginnings and endings
we reach through it all,
we fight through it all,
we love through it all,
again and again
we start over
again and again,
again and again.

Writing prompt selecting the 4th chapter (4 month) and the 5th (5th day) paragraph. Selecting 5 words from that chapter: *relationships, purpose, belief, intimacy, weave,* from the book *Belonging: Remembering Ourselves Home* by Toko-pa Turner.

Intimacy Creates a Weaving of Souls

intimacy creates a
weaving of souls
a place where what
we think is purpose
falls away
the belief of who we are
is abandoned at
the sacredness of just being
what we are learning
at this time of purpose
is to let it all drift away
as it must
in the eyes of seeing
what really matters
in our relationship with humanity
not built on the poverty
of our emptiness
but through the richness of love
that has been hidden
from our hearts
through selective purpose
what weighs heavy on us
is lifted now

shedding layers that do not
belong to us
ways that crack the between spaces
that weave us into the whole
we are naked now
as our tears are the same
the belief systems that we
thought carried us
are not the true releasing
of our walking way
we are made of love and light
touching our truths
through compassion
this is our purpose that
weaves through us now
this is our intimate calling

Take a Deep Breath Now

take a deep breath now
at the shallows end
lay my tears down
by the river's bed
lay my prayers now
by the river's bed
one foot in the shadows
one hand in the light
rise your slanted eyes sun
melt into my night
days fold into to other days
lay my heart now
by the river's bed
take a deep breath now
at the shallows end
one soul in the shadows
one soul in the light
hand in hand with bravery
opening my eyes now
seeing through the sheltered sky
take a deep breath now
at the shallows end
one foot in the shadows
one hand in the light
I will carry you with me
I will hold you with me
spirit to spirit
life to life
one foot in the shadows
one hand in the light
it all melts and blends now

into day and into night
one foot in the shadows
one hand in the light
one soul in the shadows
one soul in the light
we will find each other
together we will fight
entering into our light now
entering into our light.

Full Pink Moon Blessings.

Pink Moon Swells Brightly

pink moon swells brightly
her eyes melancholy
tears rain
tender stars upon us
what seems to be tearing
at the seams
of our world
surreal
visceral
beneath us lies
the void
the gap
of uncertainty
of unknowing
create me a bridge
across the world
across the universe
across the sky moon
lighting the darkness
that takes us
away from us
let the movement of
our conscious effort
come
even in stillness
even in the quiet of
our silent cries

center of the heart moon
come
center of the heart earth
come
find our inner healing
touch the living light
that surrounds us
that is in us
that is us
our equal exchange towards
compassion
towards humanity
to the belonging
of our true selves
create me a bridge
to you
build me a bridge
to the universe
connecting souls forever
what was…
is no longer here
finding the new
always new…
pink moon swells brightly
her eyes melancholy
tears rain
tender stars
upon us
build now a bridge of hope
create now a bridge of love
to you
to the world
to the galaxies.

Possibilities

exquisite unfolding of
your beauty before me
I close my eyes to catch
the fragrance of your opening
the possibilities arise in me
if I let them come
and set me free
see in a child's eyes
the secret surprise
of writing healing notes
catching rainbows
through the windows
of our world now
windows now closed
but the heart of home
can fold into love
when I embrace the day
and birds wings grace
the early morning sky
I will not hesitate
to come to my heart speak
with love that now waits
for if in waiting now
I close my eyes
and prayers are on my breath
as our worlds now collide
create a day that
holds the collective of it all
in the resting song
when days are long

we can enter into
this life
belonging
only to love
belonging to the power
of brilliant light
exquisite unfolding of
your beauty before me
though every day seems
to be on repeat
it can be more than that
the possibilities arise in me
if I let them come
and set me free
and set me free
and
set
me
free.

Writing prompt from the book: *Living Beautifully with Uncertainty and Change* by Pema Chödrön.

"Bodhisattva vow, it is a commitment to dedicate our lives to keeping our hearts open and minds open and to nurturing our compassion with the longing to ease the suffering of the world."

Bodhisattva

Bodhisattva
I
long
to
embrace
the
endless
stretch
of
humanity
what
is
my
compass
to
love
is
it
coming
through
the
other

side
of
suffering?
Bodhisattva
suffering
glimpses
behind
chaos
I
am
open
to
shelter
you
in
my
heart
space
cradling
prayers
to
sacred
ground
Bodhisattva
groundlessness
opens
the
grounding
of
compassion
love's
wide
expanding

from
my
heart
to
ease
your
pain
your
ache
hold
your
tears
as
my
own
Bodhisattva
vow
to
love.

A Vignette.

Colors

I fell into blue
clouds waiting for an
invitation to sleep,
waiting and wanting to just
receive a resting call to lay endlessly

white horizons touching
edges of dreams entering
into a stream of dancing snowflakes
covering the spring ground
where winter's breath rests on

yellow daffodils that
rise in my garden settling
against trees that
skim the sullen sky
with weaving branches of

green movement in the wind
rustling and still at the
same time coming to their
bold bursting into the

red sunset that melts the
snow finding and knowing
its secret moment to move
into the deep widening

black night that shelters our
restless thoughts with a
resting call to
receive an invitation to just sleep.

Writing prompt: Line from an article by Julio Vincent Gambuto, "Prepare for The Ultimate Gaslighting."

"I hope you might consider this: what happened is in-explicably incredible. It's the greatest gift unwrapped. Not the deaths, not the virus but the 'Great Pause.'"

The "Great Pause"

the "great pause"
requiring the existential
dialing back of our movement
pushing us inward
not only in our homes
but in our souls
life altering
bending the curve of the
true spiraling of our lives
humanity came to its halt
of rushing and remained
conscious of life
of family
of cleaning
of teaching
of reading
of being
of watching our
world's unexpected falling
but we came to holding
the earth more gently
as we also rise with
great prayer
great acts

great compassion
great giving
for healing in this
"great pause"
what settled inside of us
settled the earth
to grow
to heal
to live
we will come out of
the other end of this
with chances of
new choice
new voice
new living
from our beings
crying now from the crack
in our bold living
we lived large
we bought large
we expected
large and constant
movement from us
as stores always do
they will enter our psyche
with their come back sales
their Black Friday sales
their after the dust settle sales
their false hope
getting us back to living
our false lives
we found holy
between the darkness and
the healing of the earth

and the earth smiled
and for a while as this
dark moment fell upon
our history
in our time
we experienced
"the great pause."

Writing prompt: *A Found Poem*, a Cento using titles of some of the books I have on my shelves and creating them into a poem.

A Found Poem

"Woman of Spirit"
"awaken woman
 unearth yourself
 worship your truth"
"land"
"wild"
 with
"purple hibiscus"
 I will ride
"blue horses"
 an "Invitation"
 towards the
"West Wind"
"As Easy as Breathing"
"Incandescent"
"Blue Clouds"
 with a "Thirst"
 to find my
"Journey of the Heart"
"Road less Traveled"
 coming to my
"Soul Shaping"
 My "Lamentations of the Sea"
 in me
 to bring me

"Where Journeys Meet"
 finding my
"Hidden Lights"
"What We Ache For"
"Living Beautifully with Uncertainty and Change"
 finding "The Call"
"Poetry as a Spiritual Practice"
"My Reclamation Song"
"The Bell and The Black Bird"
 the sound of "Belonging"
"remembering ourselves home"
"When Things Fall Apart"
 find my "Periscope Heart"
"To Bless This Space Between Us"
"The Seasons of the Soul"
 and opening
"With Gratitude and Grace"

 Words are not mine, a collection of titles,
 "A Found Poem."

Writing prompt inspired by the *Courage Through Poetry* session with author and poet David Whyte.

The Ritual of My Being

the ritual of my being
allow sleep
with soul dreams
sweep
me clean
for the new day
if I catch with my eye
from me inside
see the spirit bird rise red
against gray skies deep in thought
deep in thought
with the holy way
healing the
ritual of my being
allow sleep
with soul dreams
sweep
me clean
for the new day
my echo
my shadow
fold into who I was
who I am
lay and spreading
across the horizon of me
if I catch with my ear
listening deep

to the voice
rising inside of me
ritual of my being
allow change
to rearrange
my mundane
and ordinary
resist
to just rotely exist but
sweep
me clean
for the new day
see the spirit bird rise red
against gray skies deep in thought
my echo
my shadow
my folding into who I was
who I am
laying and spreading
across the horizon of me
ritual of my being
allow sleep
with soul dreams
sweep
me clean
for the new day.

10 rhyming couplets with an ending.

Let Us Become

what is life's most perfect reward
what connects us and breaks the cord

step by step, gifts of life come
when stripped away naked, no one has won

the life force within us holds the gift
looking for gold in dirt as we sift

silence the breaking, soothe the ache
the more we give, the less we take

bring it to simple, bring it to pause
bring it to life's most human cause

the flower's bloom breathes out life
echoing our pain, echoing our strife

find in the shadows of our deep
where holy tears pray as we weep

in love we find hope, in hope we find grace
holding our hearts, to love's tender embrace

hold the world now, change has now come
when stripped away naked, no one has won

enter into our light, darkness has come
the arch of the rainbow, the setting of the sun

bringing our lives, to finally become
let us become,
let us become,
let us become.

Create Me a Kaleidoscope
of Colors

C reate me a kaleidoscope of colors, brilliant falling onto the waiting earth, with reds that fold into wings that sing the song of rising free in the waking morning. I catch blue with my eyes and with surprise, iridescently cracks the sky with yellows slipping between ethereal clouds of rest. I rest between the closing of winter's cold still, letting it melt over spring with brilliant green and trees that swish and sway in the afternoon rain. Magical rain filling earth's roots, filling its thirst for flourishing. For in this significant and often repeating moment, my eyes breathe in the beauty more, capture the movement of it all into my soul, into the holy resting place of my heart. Create me a kaleidoscope of colors, brilliant falling through the emptiness of my being, into this moment of now.

If I Fall into Grief

if I fall into grief
trying to find my way home
if I am in disbelief
trying to find my way to hope
home
with rooms in my heart
some bare and dark
seeking the light of day
to clear the way
to lifting the windows
in my soul
push them up and let
the breath of love in
even when I want to board them up
and sink deep inside and hide
hope
that in this moment now
without the chatter from others
of how it all should be done
how my life should be lived
sometimes I can barely breathe
what breaks the irrational
when the irrational becomes rational
when abnormal becomes the new normal
spilling out its grief
hope comes with
a tender way
bearing witness to my grief
comes with healing
turning my grief
into compassion

as we all
fold into the same place
I will not let bitterness
replace it all
even in my sorrow
find my way home
lift the windows up
let love flood in
where if even in deep
aloneness
I will find who I am
love me
hold
me
be kind to
me
through my vulnerable
as I watch it turn
into my strength
to heal my crying places
as love comes
love always comes.

Writing prompt: Title of one of my favorite authors and book: *Bless The Place Between Us* by John O' Donohue.

"Bless The Space Between Us" and the 17 line from the 17 page: "the unfinished and the unsolved."

Our Surrendering Pause

"bless the space between us"
 the clear and unwanted gap
 that holds our confused silence
 in our surrendering pause

"the unfinished and the unsolved"
 let the waiting time dissolve
 something new is emerging
 setting the broken butterfly free

 the glances and the glimpse at our lives
 no more racing by in a rush
 stir the heart to meet the other's eyes
"bless the space between us"

 I wake with a haunting
 an awakening to sinking into today
 I slip between dreams and eyes opening
 all is still "the unfinished and the unsolved"
 but all is always "the unfinished and the unsolved"

 so I "bless this space between us"
 with holy prayers for our aching souls

when I cradle the day in serenity
releasing all what I cannot control
with breath, with pause, with making us whole.

Where Pause Meets Doing

bending to the day
where pause meets doing
and doing meets pausing
the delicate balance
of what is best
for you right now
when your eyes with wonder
see the grace of day
as it's unfolding
when you see the thin line break
falling this way or that
both ways are held in love
for when the day splits
and spills into your heart
hold the sorrow of it
hold the moments of
the beauty of it
the sun lifts the sky high
above us with brightness
to remind us of light
the evening, the calling night
breath of black
reminds us of
the stillness of the dark
in the silence of it
we seek refuge
lean into this day
where pause meets doing
and doing meets pausing
the delicate balance
of what is best

for you right now
when you see the thin line break
falling this way or that
both ways are held in love
tears
laughter
vulnerable
brave
feeling undone
and put together again
all of this is held in love
for when the day splits
and spills into your heart
make room
for compassion
make room
for gentleness
make room
for love
to hold you
as you are right now.

A conversation with John O'Donohue, a favorite writer and poet of mine. Taking excerpts from his book, *Anam Cara: A book of Celtic Wisdom* and poems from his book, *To Bless the Space Between Us* and having a conversation with 4 parts of 4 of my poems:

"She Scooped Up Today"

"Life in Its Transparency"

"Love Comes for Us"

"Live a Life"

A Conversation with John O'Donohue

JOHN:
"May this morning of innocent beginning,
When the gift within you slips clear
Of the sticky web of the personal
With its hurt and its hauntings,
And fixed fortress corners,"
To Bless the Space Between Us—
Poem: "For The Artist At The Start Of Day"

MAUREEN:
she clothes herself in morning
holding the glistening line
between dark and light
rising from a bed of sunrise
catching blue sky as sacred
as sacred as opening her eyes.
Poem: She Scooped Up Today

JOHN:

"We are lonely and lost in our hungry transparency.
We desperately need a new and gentle light where
the soul can shelter and reveal its ancient
belonging."
Anam Cara

MAUREEN:

life in its transparency
we hold the veils
that layer us
sometimes dark and mysterious
holding our soul inward.
Poem: "Life In Its Transparency"

JOHN:

"In the vast universe that often seems sinister and
unaware of us, we need the presence and shelter of
love to transfigure our loneliness."
Anam Cara

MAUREEN:

love comes for us
comes when the fray of life pains us
love comes for us
even when we are curled and
lying on the earth of our grief.
Poem: "Love Comes For Us."

JOHN:

"May you arise each day with a voice
Of blessing whispering in your heart
May you find harmony between your soul and life
May the sanctuary of your soul
never become haunted.
To Bless the Space Between Us—
Poem: "For Belonging"

MAUREEN:

live a life
human to spirit
breathing in all of it
whatever grieves you
whatever lives right through you
and you live right through it.
Poem: "Live A Life."

Writing prompt: From the wonderful workshop with author and poet David White, *Courage Through Poetry*.

My poem today is about some things he talked about with us yesterday. To *"ask the questions without knowing the answers, to have that courageous conversation with yourself. It is an invitation, asking ourselves the questions that can make or unmake ourselves."*

Heart Speak

heart speak
when the din of my
outer world fades
fades into a silent space
within me
"an invitation to ask the courageous question"
asking myself
questions that can
"make or unmake me"
our sheltering
let us scatter our outer thoughts
to the fire
"like notes written"
and tossed into the flame
fear
hoarding
anxiety driven
too much doing
just enough to hide
from our true selves
let it all fall to the flame

breaking away
from the definition
of what the world
wants me to be
who I truly am
the deep horizon of me
with vast wide edges
that hold the sacredness of me
from the beginning
"the courageous conversation" came
deep
coming to my heart space
listen
breathe and listen…
intuitive
brave and wanting me
to have heart
take heart
coming to my
compassionate being
heart speak
when I see the parallel lives
I live
sink deep into my
heart center
when the din of my
outer world fades
I come into my
silent place to have a
"courageous conversation"
I come to my heart speak.

What Waits at My Doorstep

seeing life
what waits at my doorstep
invited
uninvited
what remains
visible
invisible
seeing through a
different lens
the between of it
reaching and pulling
this way or that
sitting in the middle
of it
like the eye of a storm
silent in its waiting
but it always surrenders
to the bluest of skies
what waits at my doorstep
invited
uninvited
I stretch out my hands
cupping the ache of it
what creates
perseverance
hope
faith
in this unbelievable point
of time
what remains

visible
invisible
seeing with the
eyes of the soul
what tries to become
my weakness
through fear
becomes my unformidable strength
because we seek
love to become
our brave
conquering what
is uninvited
dropping into the silent point
dropping in the middle way
a place of our holy pause
and seeing wholly
with compassion
what becomes my invitation
to the door of my heart
becoming wide open
the visible
becoming love
being love
seeing love
for myself,
for the world.

Earth Moon, New Moon

earth moon
new moon
what replenishes
the womb
of mother earth
comes to replenish
the inner landscape
of our true nature
emerging through the soil
through the landscape
of dark and light
landscape of our recovery
new moon
earth moon
sifting through what
never belonged to us
guardians of earth life
we are…
protecting what thrives
all around us
in us
into a spiraling new beginning
even in our catastrophe
the earth is birthing
even in our own unearthing
our narratives have changed
we find strength in who we are
shedding what was
into a new and brilliant earth
earth moon

new moon
let healing come
soul to body
earth to moon
dark to light
the universe within us
expanding within us
to touch the ever-expanding
galaxy of life
the spiritual roots
of our tending
flourishing comes to beginnings
by embracing
the new moon
a new earth
a new life
under the surface
patience waits
as we listen to
the reverb of life
echoing past existences
let us find our heart way
to bear witness
in this place of borrowed time
finding our deep
within holy ground
new earth
new moon
new me
if this tragic experience
transforms us
the breathing earth sings
impossible healing has come

the antidote to living is
seeing with true sight
living with new lives
to protect each other
to protect the earth
in the great collective
of our inner belonging
earth moon
new moon.

Writing prompt: Yesterday was not only Earth Day, but it was the New Moon.

Every new moon I pick a rune, an oracle, an announcing for my life. This New Moon's rune was: Fertility, New Beginnings. (How fitting right?).

This rune's meaning is akin to the Moon, the intuitive part of nature. The urge for harmonizing relationships. The completion of beginnings finding a joyful deliverance to a new path, a great power. This rune signals your emergence from a closed and chrysalis state and receiving release from tension and uncertainty. This rune is so fitting not only for me but for you. Immerse yourself into these words, freeing yourself, flying free.

This is a 10 stanza haiku.

Sphere of Life Living

natural waiting
tender seed deep in dark moon
soaked with clothing rain

urge to move forward
feet sink deep into my path
hesitant longing

sphere of life living
harmonizing compassion
even to myself

signaling newness
eyes steal the sphere of brightness
moon floods my soul path

ache keeps me silent
tears fall upon emerging
flowers seek sunlight

disappear dark thoughts
resting on each silent breath
see life from my heart

come new beginnings
pain becomes my threshold now
my expanding life

release uncertain
clear rises with each new dawn
life's expectations

chrysalis waiting
comes with deep contemplation
comes from moving through

cocooned deep within
painted by the brush of God
butterfly fly free

Writing prompt: This prompt is based on one of my favorite bands and truly one of my favorite songs, "Bad" by U2.

Even though the meaning of this song is based on heroin addiction, it touches close to home having lost a brother to addiction with co-morbid conditions this past summer, that took his life because of heroin. I'm taking a different twist on it.

I am using the lines: "I'm wide awake, I'm not sleeping."

This poem is dedicated to the nurses and doctors on the front lines who are fighting for our lives against the Coronavirus. I see you, even when others protest against you and call you fake. Many who might as well be sticking the needle in their arm, not taking this boundless, ferocious disease seriously. I see you, "I am wide awake."

If I See through the Broken Sky

if I see
through the
broken sky
weight of life
heavy
wings broken
can't fly
if I look away
shut myself off
hit the ground
in this endless fray
I lay

myself
down
down
down
to holy ground
only to rise
and pray
"I'm wide awake
I'm not sleeping"
in my aloneness
my groundlessness
my restlessness
my emptiness
I still see you
because
"I'm wide awake, I'm not sleeping"
I see your
ripped open heart
pain in your eyes
when all you do
is fight for our lives
when others despise
you
I will lift you high
I see the compassion
through your eyes
what rages
against us
you still fight
for us
you take care
of us
you will sit with us
when our last moment ends

and you hold our hands
with our last dying breath
this seemingly endless death
when I hit
desperation
in isolation
you receive
condemnation
giving us liberation
seeing
life's creation
receiving
sacred redemption
for I will rise
in this endless fray
I lay myself
down
down
down
on the floor
and I will pray
"I'm wide awake
I'm not sleeping"
I see your cause
in this mighty pause
trying not to let
life slip away
I lay down and pray
I'll speak for you
light my candle for you
your endless will
through this crying still
and from my window sill
I will shout for you

I will clap for you
for all I see
when I walk the quiet streets
through this bitter strife
I see you saving a life
I see you
because
"I'm wide awake. I'm not sleeping"
no I will not
close my eyes
indulge in another man's
hating lies
again I will rise
and
rise
and
rise
"I'm wide awake
I'm not sleeping"

Healing to the World

let your soul
cry out the poem
your heart color
the canvas
your fingers
play the instrument
dance your dance
it becomes
our comfort
our memory spilling
out
of our days
our waiting way
let it pour from us
pen to phrase
of silent days
spiraling
reds and yellows
pressed against
black
swells through
the light
of us
the music note
cuts through
thick air
with peaceful melody
songs that embrace
the lyrics
that dances
on our melancholy

I take the steps
following the
beat of my drum
I hum
I write
I capture this moment
with brush strokes
upon my crying soul
I play endlessly the
notes in the consciousness
of my being
let your gifts become
your voice
your painting
telling the story
your song
soothing the heart
your poem
calming the soul
letting yourself
and others know
we find refuge
in the spirit
of who we are
sending
healing
to
the
world.

Writing prompt seeing the words "We Got This" on a front window of a home in my neighborhood while walking my dog Tsuki.

"We Got This"

slant me down
head bowed low
I rest it in dry hands
that crack and
clasp my aloneness
touching my hand to
hand in somber
prayer but holding
the words
"hang in there"
that I saw over
three weeks ago on
a large window
of a house
now taped with pieces
of construction paper
bold with encouragement
"we got this"
candle on the
stoop sitting in the
quiet rain it will be
lit again and again
vigil of heart
prayer to prayer
rising burning flame
"we got this"

I feel a crack in
my heart that I
want to slip into
but I pour my
morning coffee
and sit by the sky
lighting through my
window take my journal
in hand speaking
words on paper
that rage
against my being
but cradle
my soul in hope
at the same time
"we got this"
masks on
hands wet
with clean
and it all
seems
to be a dream
but the stares from
our eyes glazed over
with unexpectedness
intruding on our lives
"we got this"
while others fight
the front lines
to save us
one
by
one

we become
like the flame
of the candle
burning
through it
washing away
the
fear
it all comes
in
waves
but I see
our brilliant hearts
give
learn
live
love
and we
thrive
to
survive
to truly, truly know…
"we got this"

Using lines from the teachings of author and poet David White's session: *Courage Through Poetry.*

Writing Prompts:

"make a nest now"
"even to the stranger in you"
"drop the peripheral self"
"to find what will speak your name"

Bold Conversation

patience will find me
as I ease into the
heart of me
it is not always simple
to clear away
the unnecessary
I want to cling
to it
wear it as my garment
the "peripheral self"
of me
often comforts me
fear makes me
believe it protects me
"drop the peripheral self"
to have the
bold conversation
to see the silence
that settles between
dawn and light

I catch with my eye
wings of a bird
cutting through sky
"make a nest now"
in the still
of me
let the nature of it
teach me
"drop the peripheral self"
long enough to see
"the stranger in"
me
for when she comes
spilling out
before me
what does not belong
pilgrims on this journey
we are...
let me have the
bold conversation
to see the silence between
dawn and light
I catch with my eye
wings of a bird
cutting through sky
"make a nest now"
in the still
of me
"drop the peripheral self"
long enough
"to find what will speak my name"
I see it rise
from the

empty depths
of me
ready to be filled
with new
my pilgrim path
calling my journey
by name
easing into the
heart of me
yes…
"to find what will speak my name."

In early December I had the opportunity through my work to go for a brief but memorable visit to Rome, Italy. To see the empty streets caused by COVID–19 compared to the bustling streets I experience is definitely surreal.

Pieces of Italy

in early December
I came to you
majestic city Roma
with your arches
and domes
business cascading
pleasure
I held your magnificence
pieces of Italy
in my heart
silhouette landscapes
as the sun draped
the sky folding over
hills that held homes
ancient meeting modern
lifting the mystery
of your stories
pieces of Italy
the presence of the people
inviting
philosophically creating
everything was
tanto
with their welcoming

conversations through
delectable delights
Cacio e Pepe
simple and delicate
tasted with wine
and laughter
upon our waiting lips
evening candles
lit up our smiling faces
pieces of Italy
from peering through
the Aventine keyhole
breathing in
St. Peter's Basilica
the art that
spoke holy
and reverent to the
history of artists
that came and filled this
city with great memory
from the Pantheon
to the Saint Steps
still the presence of
your people
are most inviting
that gathered on
a warm December evening
near the Saint steps
while we strolled down
cobblestone-streets
spiraling with little shops
I found ornaments
hand painted

for the
Christmas tree
pieces of Italy
though brief
spoke of pure belonging
I but a visitor
in your contagiously
smiling city
with bold stories
of pain
of fame
of living
of being
opening the heart of
who you are
early December
came and went
and quickly
these moments
disappeared
now on my flight back
to Chicago
but your rich
and bold culture
filled my heart
filled my belly
seeing the beauty
of who you are
now your streets
wait in silence
to open up
your inviting hearts again
where resilience

sparks life
where ancient folds
into modern
waiting for your people
to flood the streets again
with your contagious laughter.

A 12 rhyming couplet.

Self

they say don't lean yourself, into yesterdays
become new and begin, your brand new day

who you were, who you are, always folds
a self folding into self, you tenderly hold

the ache and suffering, that came and went
the interweaving blessings, that were sent

what breaks and falls, comes to complete you
pulls away and pulls you in, only to redeem you

I will not hold onto endless sorrow
that makes its way into my tomorrows

I will hold her, cry with her, learn from her, love her
belonging coming to compassion, as I surrender

surrender to the deepest part of grace
illuminating love, humility upon my face

what pulls me through the fire, makes me stronger
letting what must go, not being that way any longer

what moves through the storm, becomes the still
what comes to complete my surviving will

will to believe in, all that I have survived
I have flourished, I have bloomed, I have thrived

for yesterdays built me, into who I am today
I rise with gratefulness, finding my heart way.

This is a Cento created from lines of each of my 29 poems for writing a new poem each day, during this pandemic and for National Poetry Month. The last line is new to complete my whole poem of 30 lines for today.

My heart is wide and filled with poetry, ready to spill into the hearts and souls of all the world.

The Last Poem

I hold water like soft tears
the rain wept lonely loss
as the grass shifts into shades of green
I spiral between
the sacredness of my being
seeing through the sheltered sky
to find our inner healing
the possibilities arise in me
embrace the endless stretch
receiving a resting call to lay endlessly
dialing back our movement
the seasons of the soul brings
the ritual of my being
enter into the light, darkness has come
create a kaleidoscope of colors
to heal my crying places
that holds our confused silence
when you see the thin line break
love comes for us

that holds the sacredness of us
in this unbelievable point of time
the landscape of our recovery
sphere of life living
weight of life heavy
let your gifts become your voice
I see our brilliant hearts
pilgrims on this journey we are
to open up our inviting hearts
a self folding into self
our surrendering pause.

ACKNOWLEDGMENTS

I wish to thank my dear sister Marianne, who has always followed and loved my poetry, who encouraged me to publish a book of my 30 Poems for April National Poetry Month, placing my footprint of poetry during this time in history; Alice Maldonado, my editor and publisher of Golden Dragonfly Press, for her swift reply to my idea of publishing these poems and co-birthing my vision to allow this book take flight quickly into the hands of many readers; Carolyn Riker, whom I give a deep bow for a beautiful and moving foreword of my poetry; my daughter Alexandra, giving me the advise of changing the title of my book to *Our Surrendering Pause*; to Reggie Kljucaric, for her honest advise about the cover of my book; to Kai Coggin, Catherine Schweig, Flora Aube, Rosemerry Wahtola Trommer, Tracy Ann Brooks for reviewing my manuscript and writing advance praises; to Lynn Pankonin Niles, a nurse in the ICU Department at Mercy Medical Center in St. Louis, a deep bow and special thank you for her endless service as a Frontline nurse through this continuing pandemic; to the doctors, nurses and essential workers that are here for us 24/7 during this pandemic; to my dog Tsuki, for her joyful antics that kept me sane through this pandemic; to all my readers, I truly thank you.

ALSO BY MAUREEN

Seasons of the Soul: Transitions and Shifts of Life,
2014

ANTHOLOGIES

*Journey of the Heart: An Anthology of Spiritual
Poetry by Women*, Catherine Ghosh, ed., 2014

Where Journeys Meet: The Voices of Women's Poetry,
Catherine Ghosh, ed., 2015

*Poetry as a Spiritual Practice: Illuminating the
Awakened Woman*, Catherine Ghosh, ed., 2016

*Hidden Lights: A Collection of Truths Not Often
Told*, Carolyn Riker & BethAnne Kapansky
Wright, eds., 2017

*Goddess: When She Rules, Expressions by
Contemporary Women*, Catherine L. Schweig, ed.,
2017

CPSIA information can be obtained
at www.ICGtesting.com
Printed in the USA
LVHW021201210221
679570LV00045B/855